Quennina Wright
The Wright Art
Harlem, N.Y.

Dear Curly Hair Cutie,

I see you struggling with bad hair day frustrations,
So I made this to help you release those tangles...
It gets better with every color!!!

Xoxo,
Curly Que

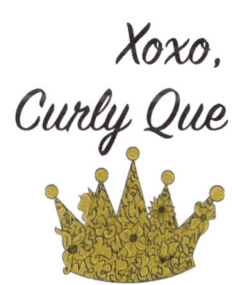

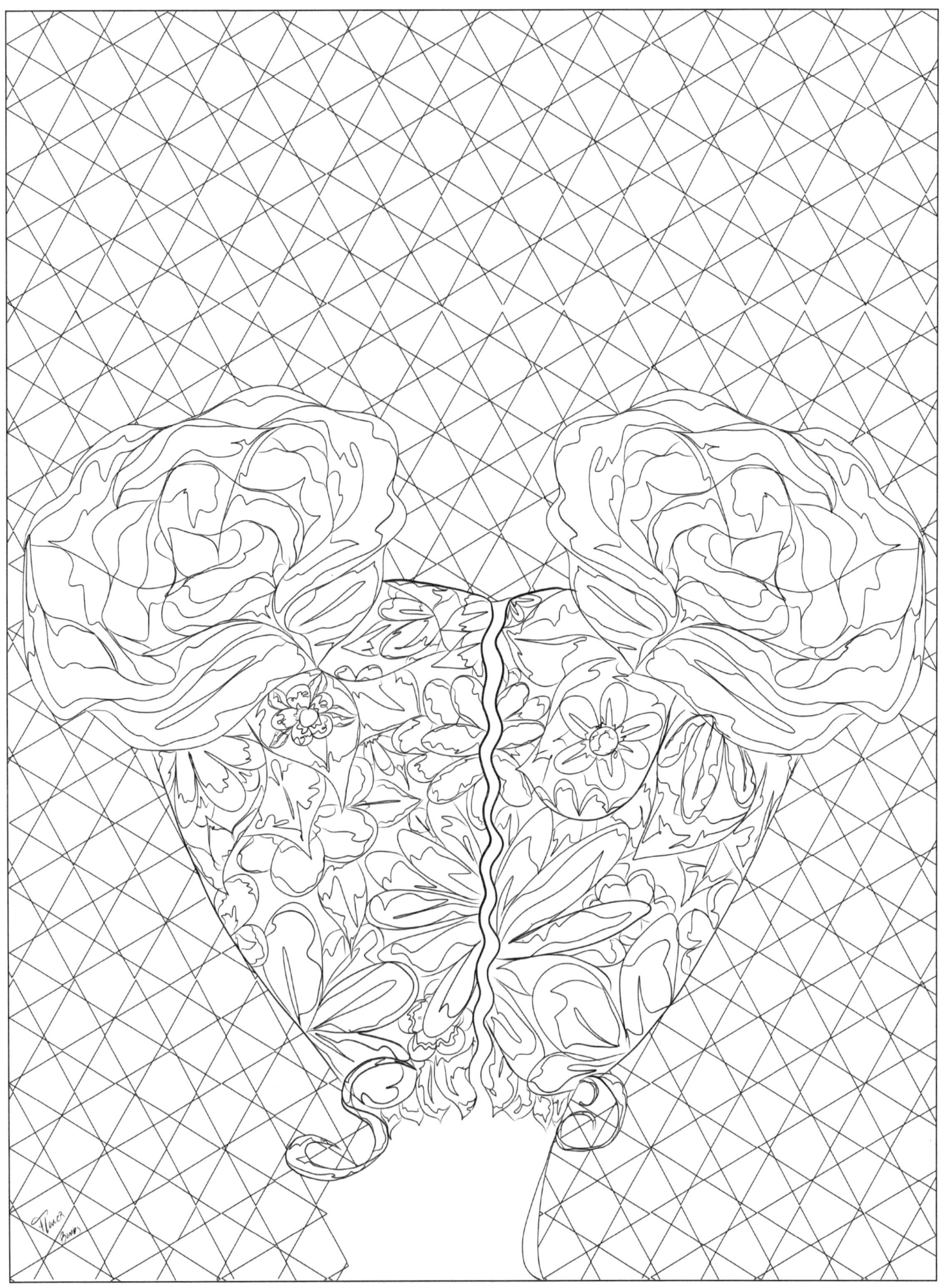

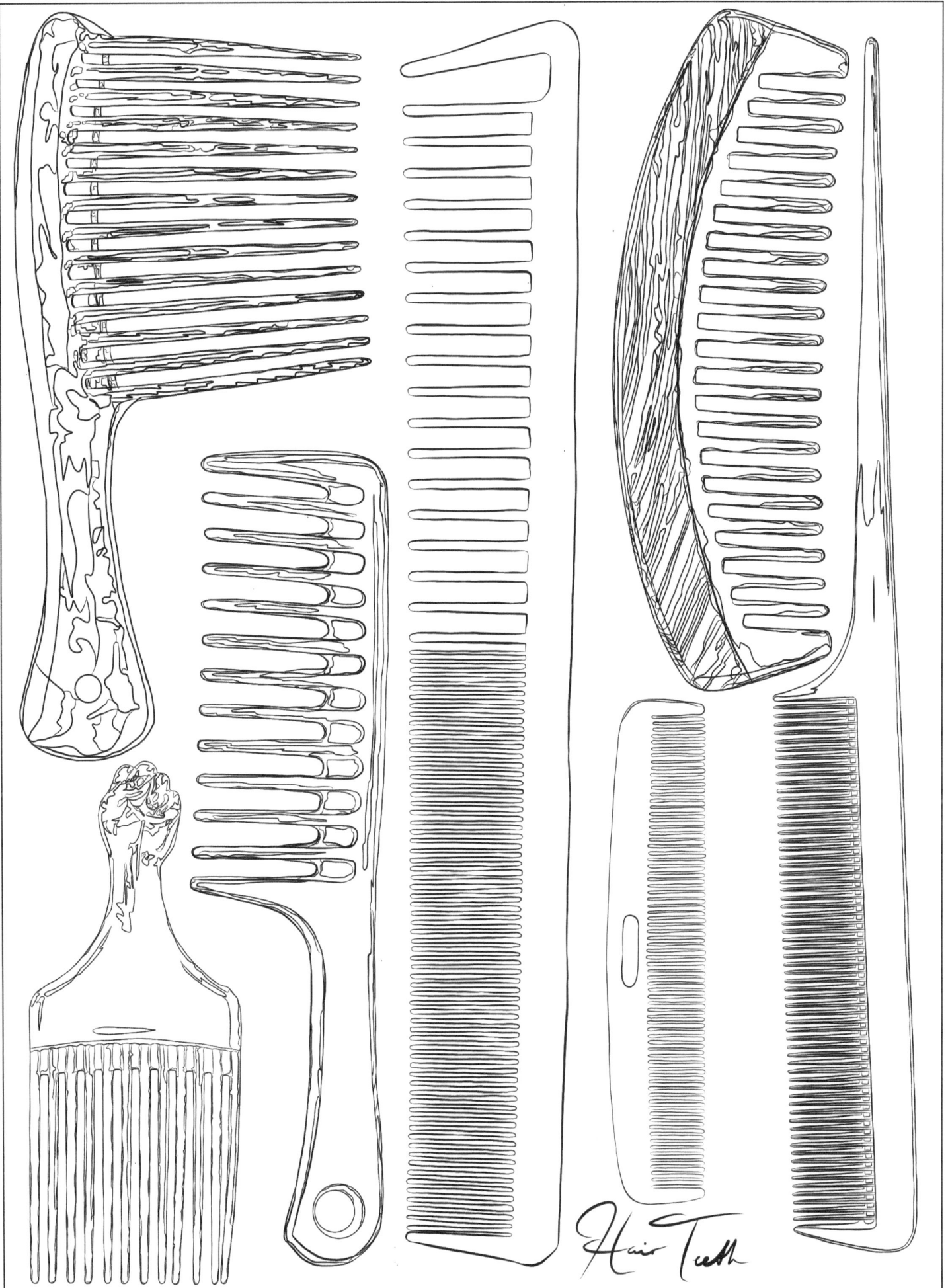

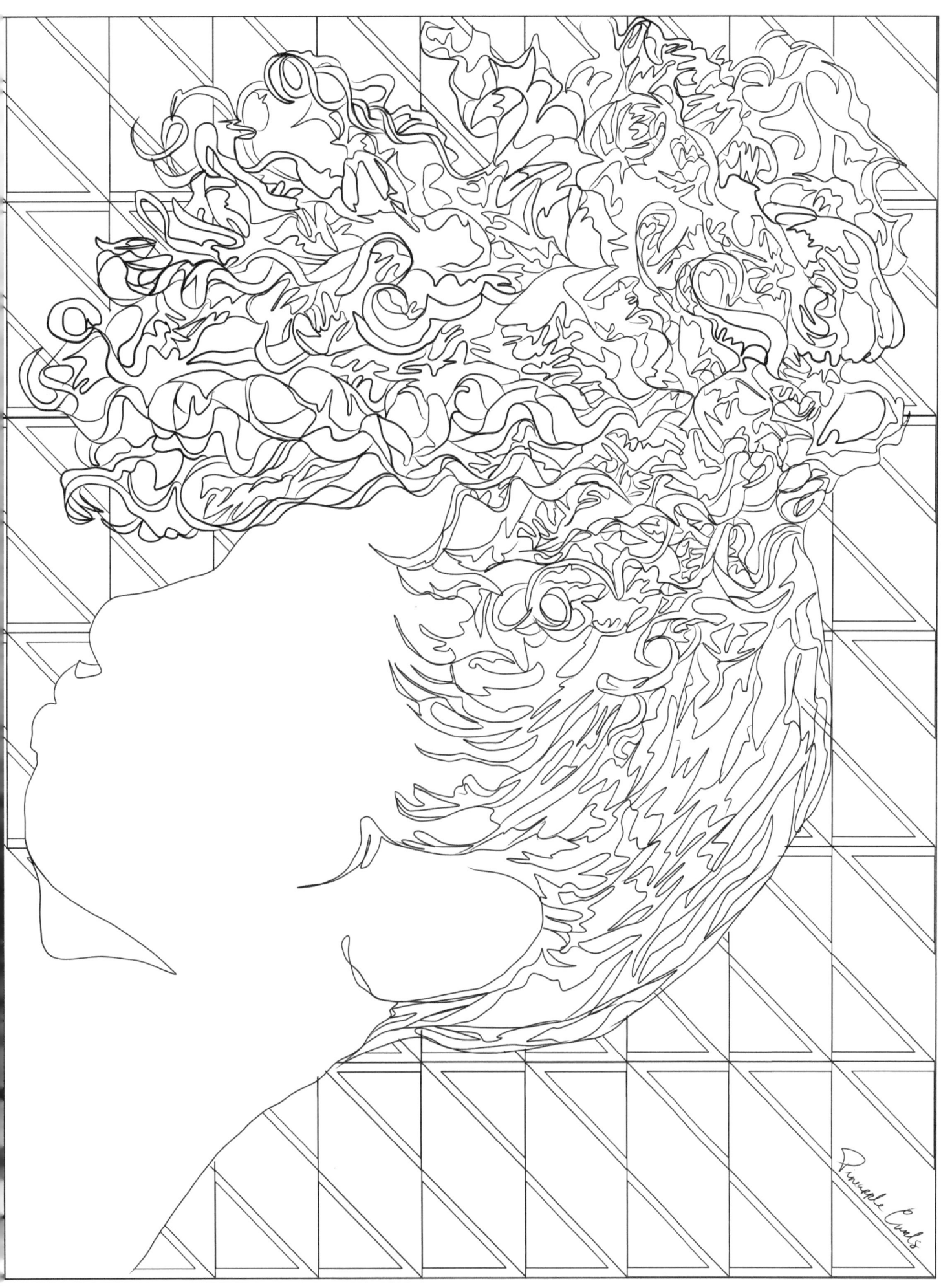

Pineapple Curls

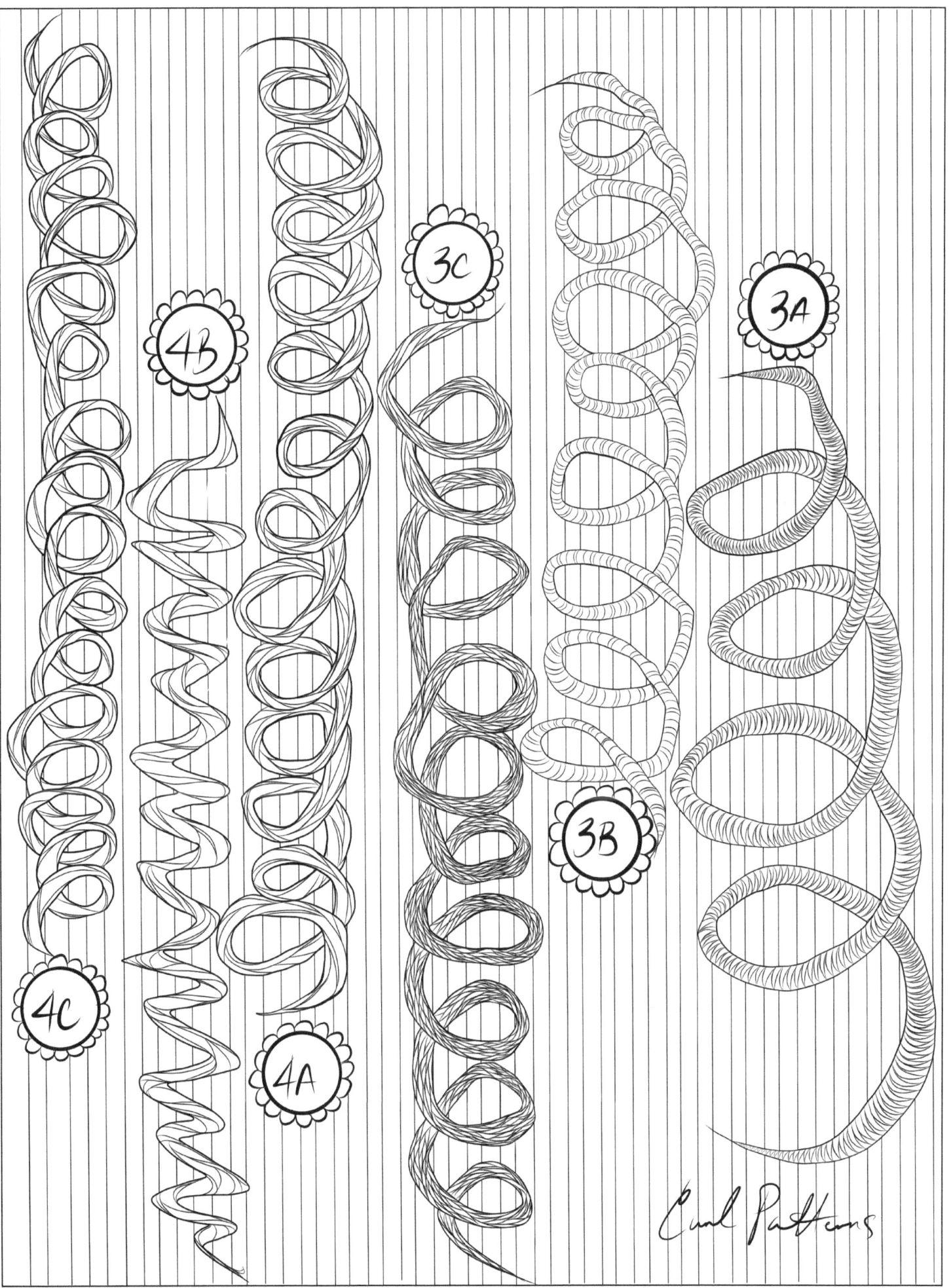

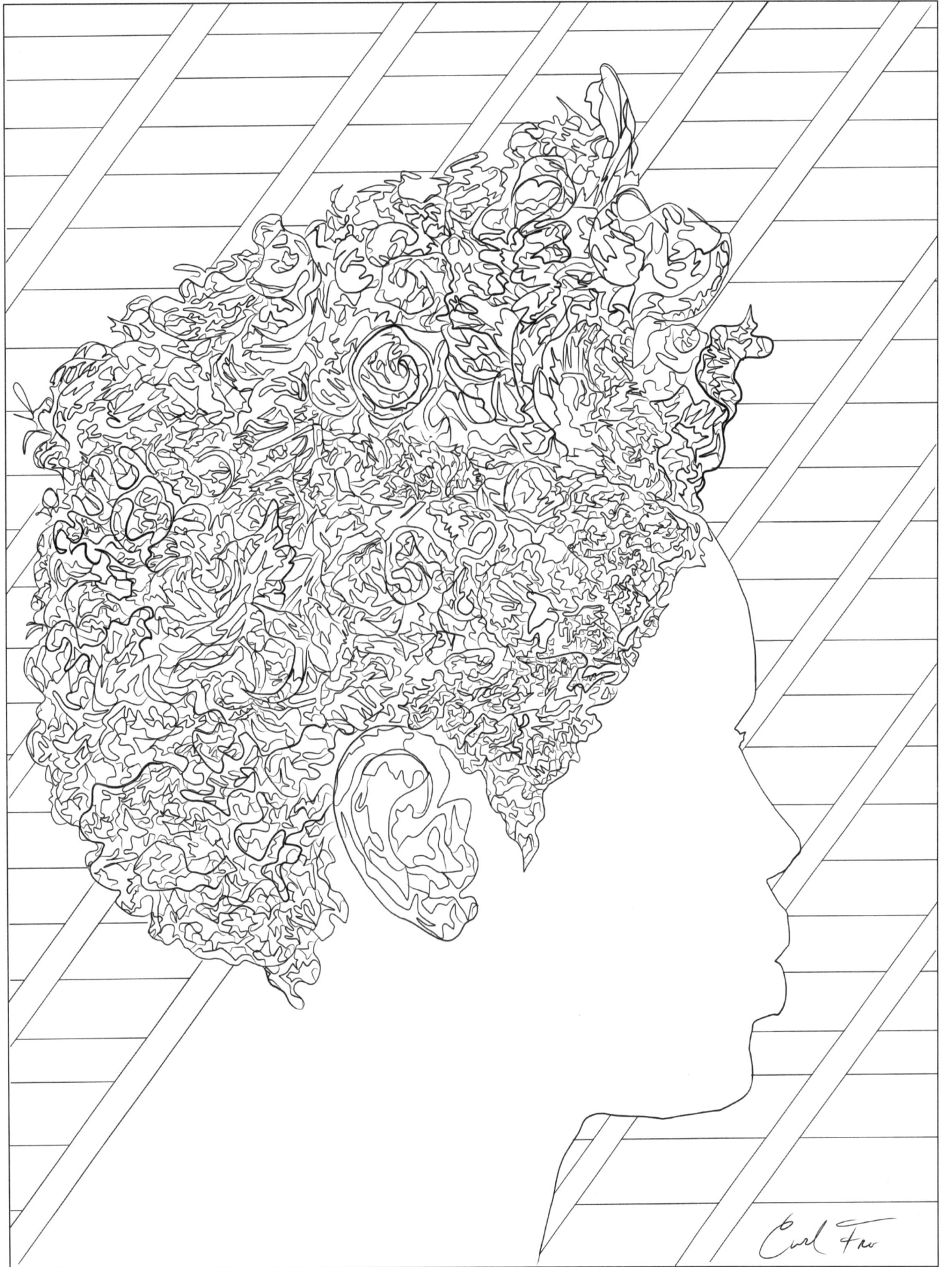

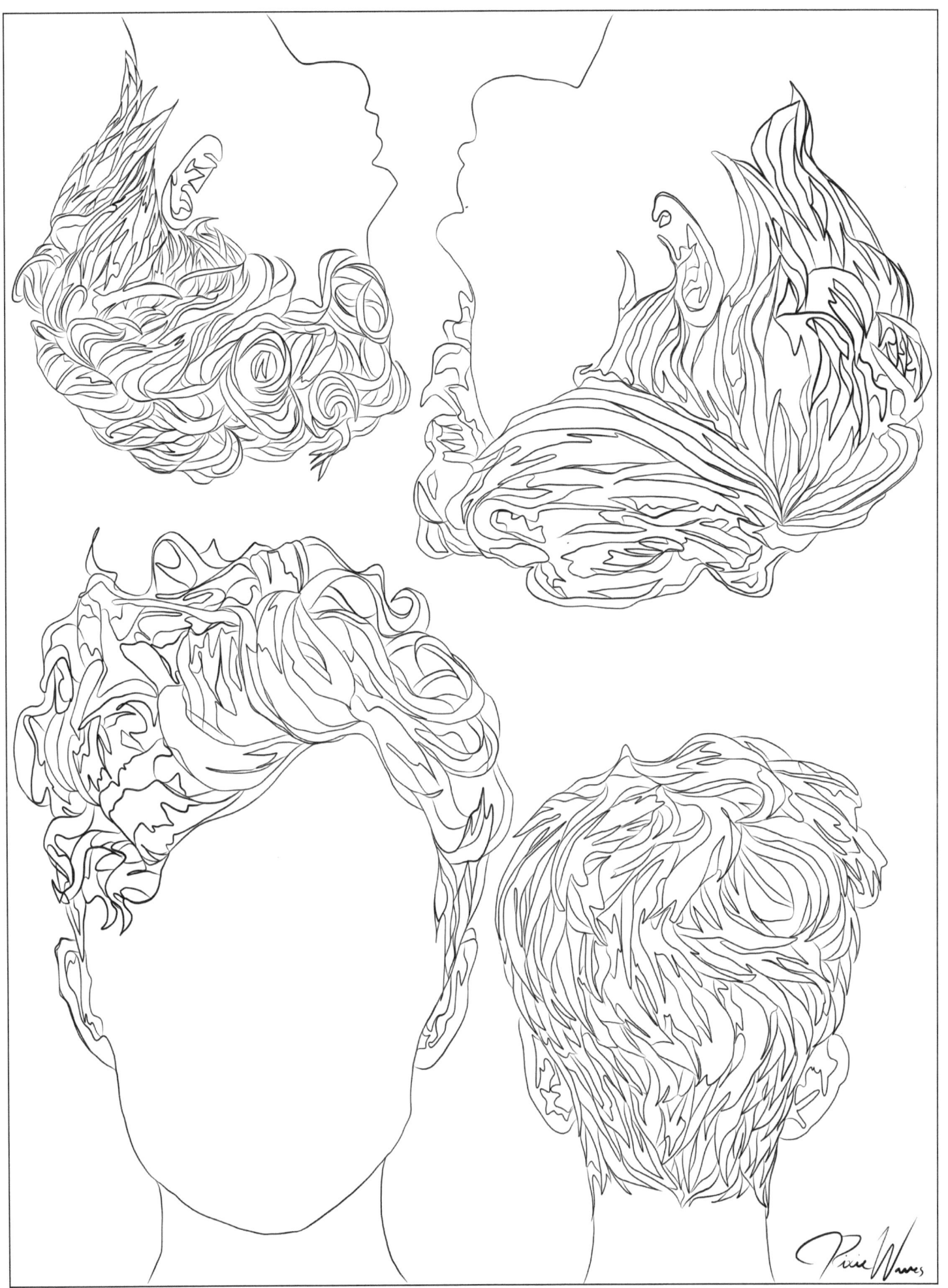

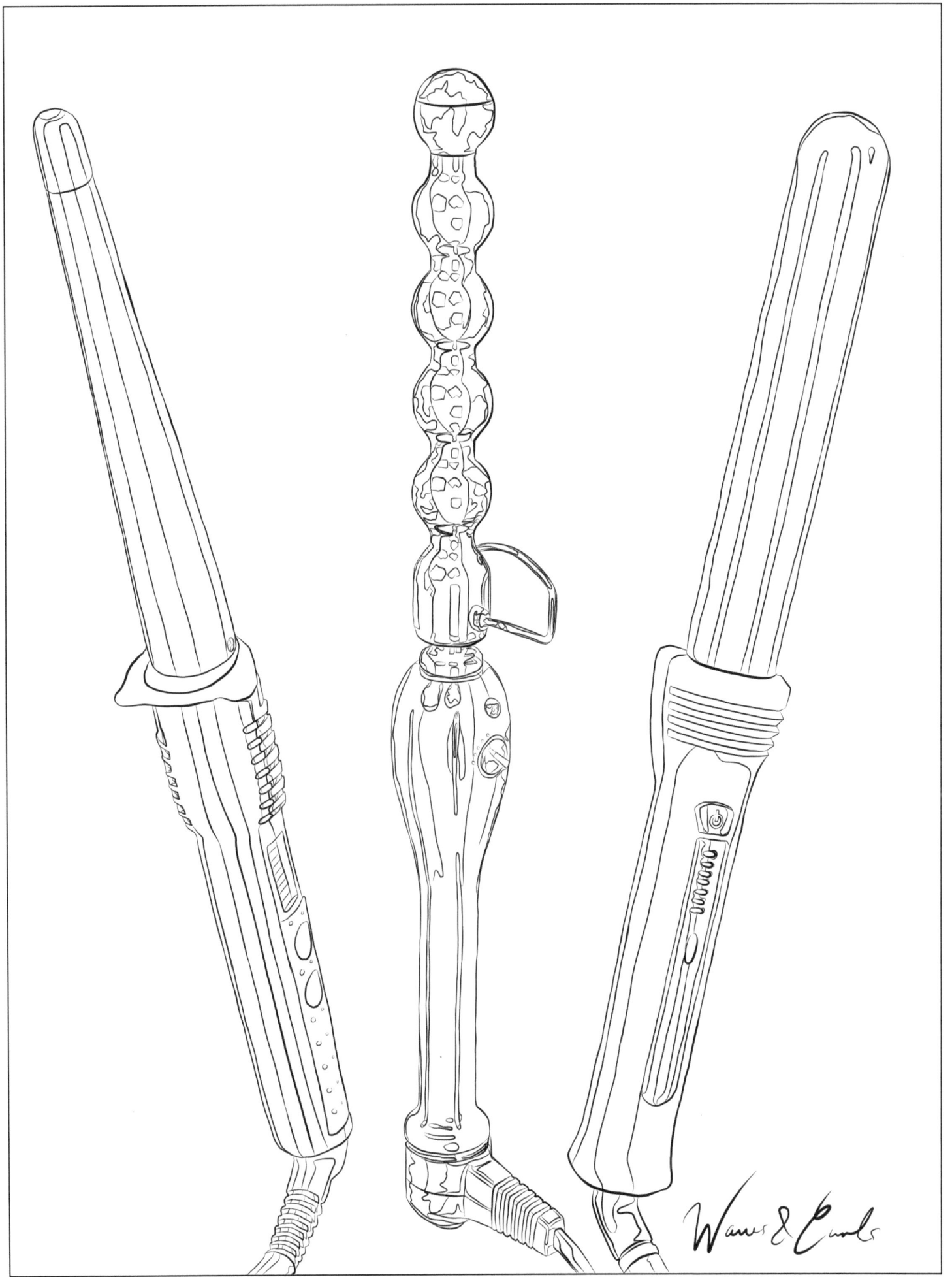

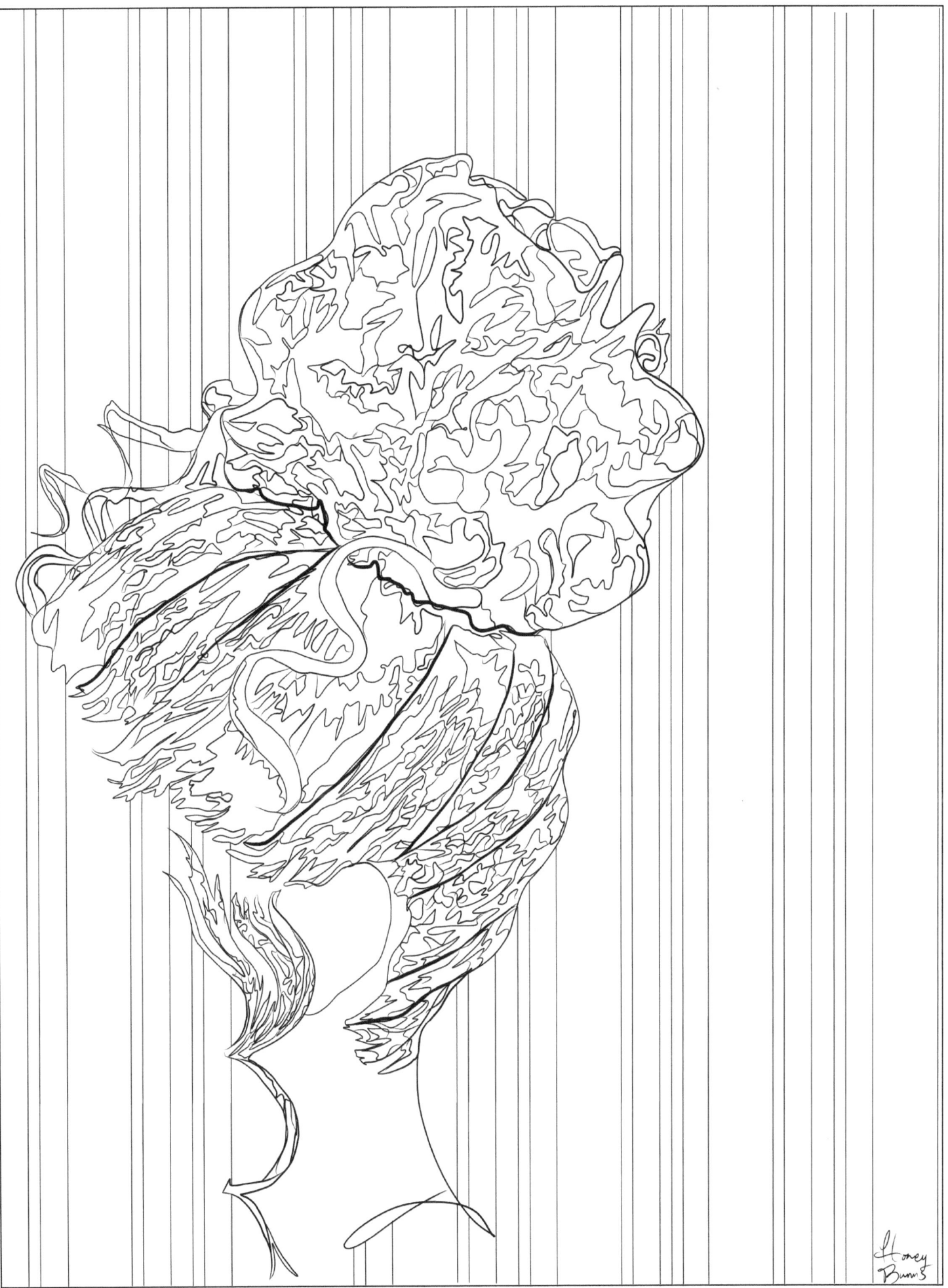

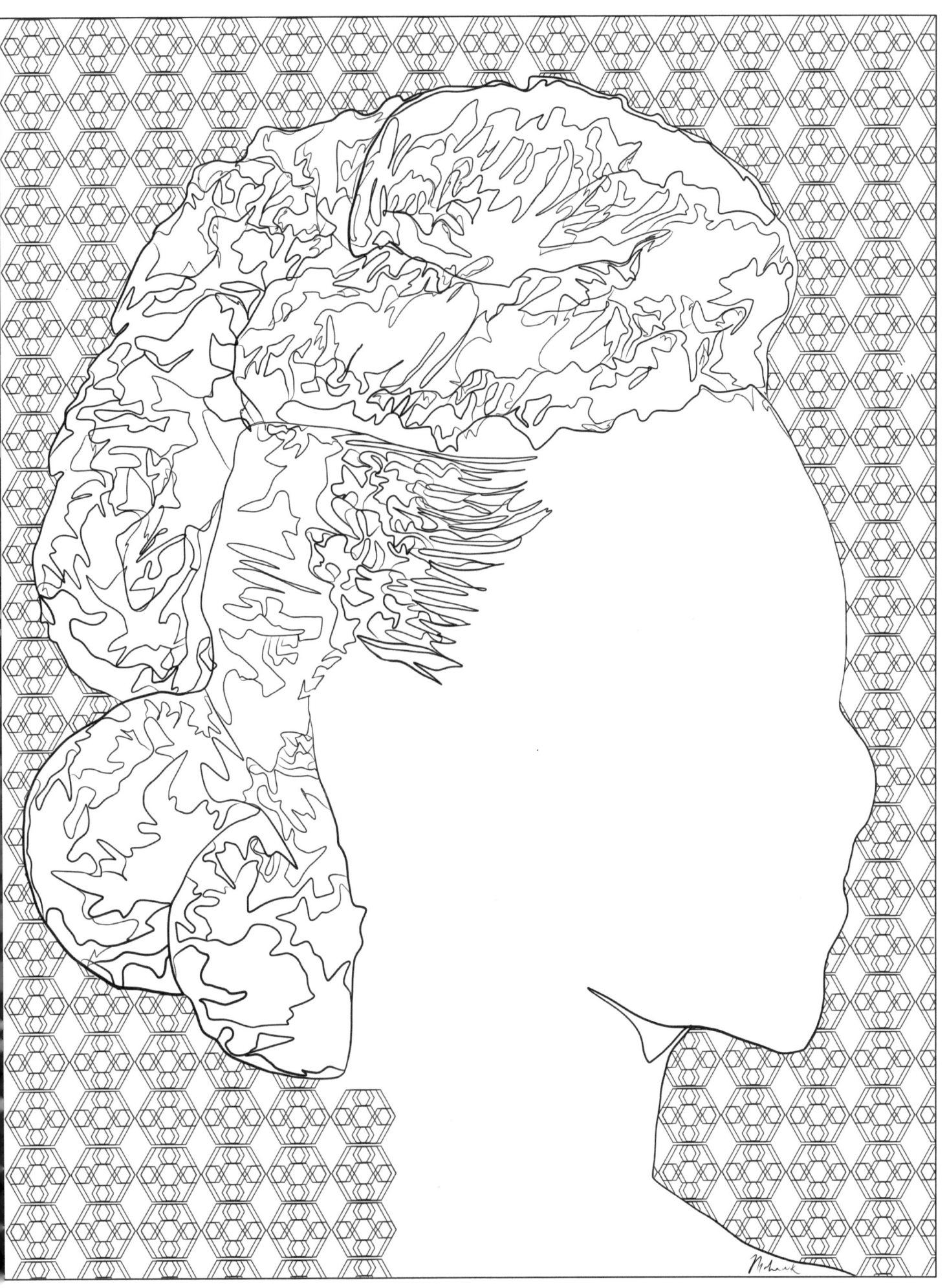

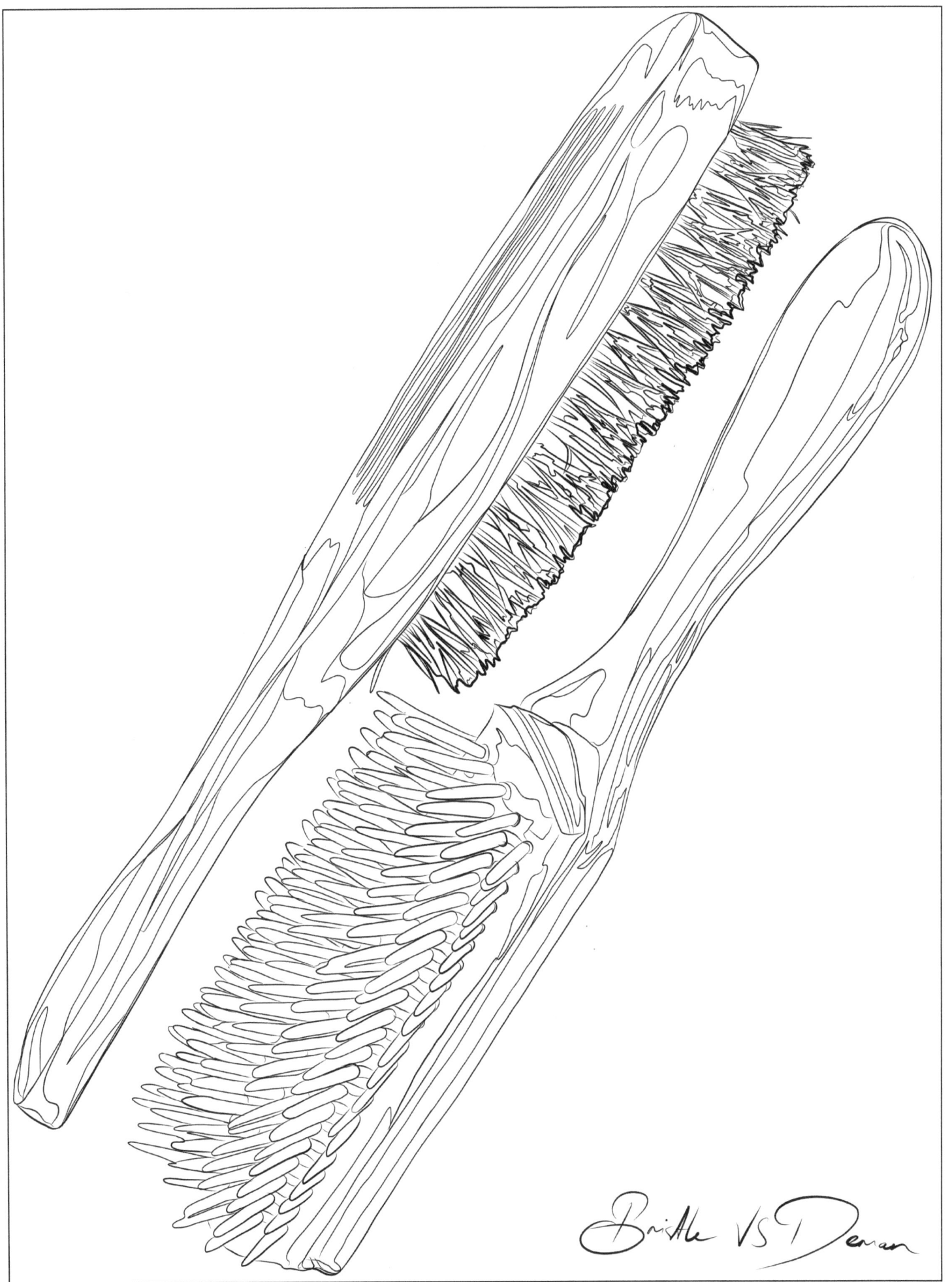

Bristle VS Denman

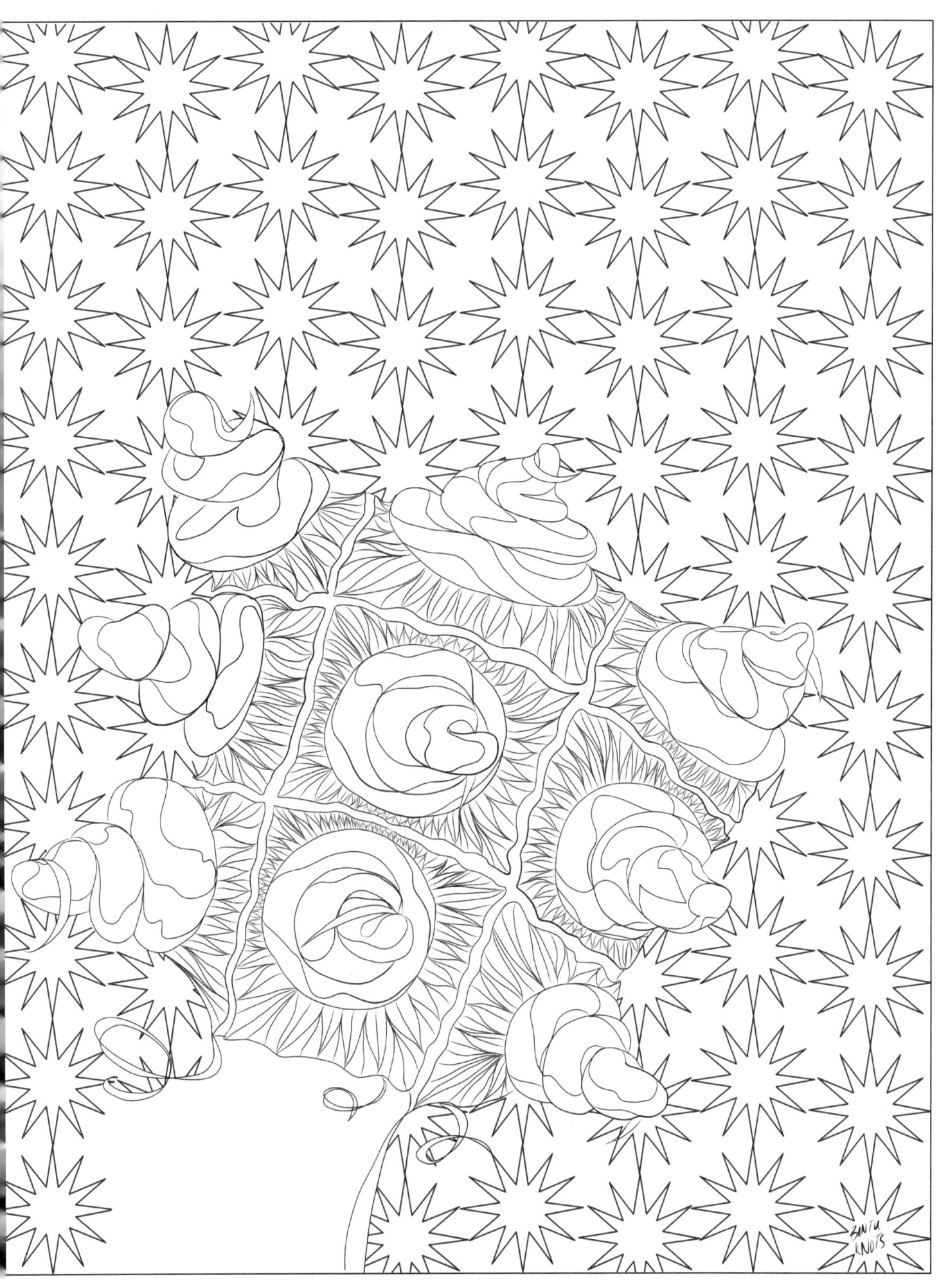

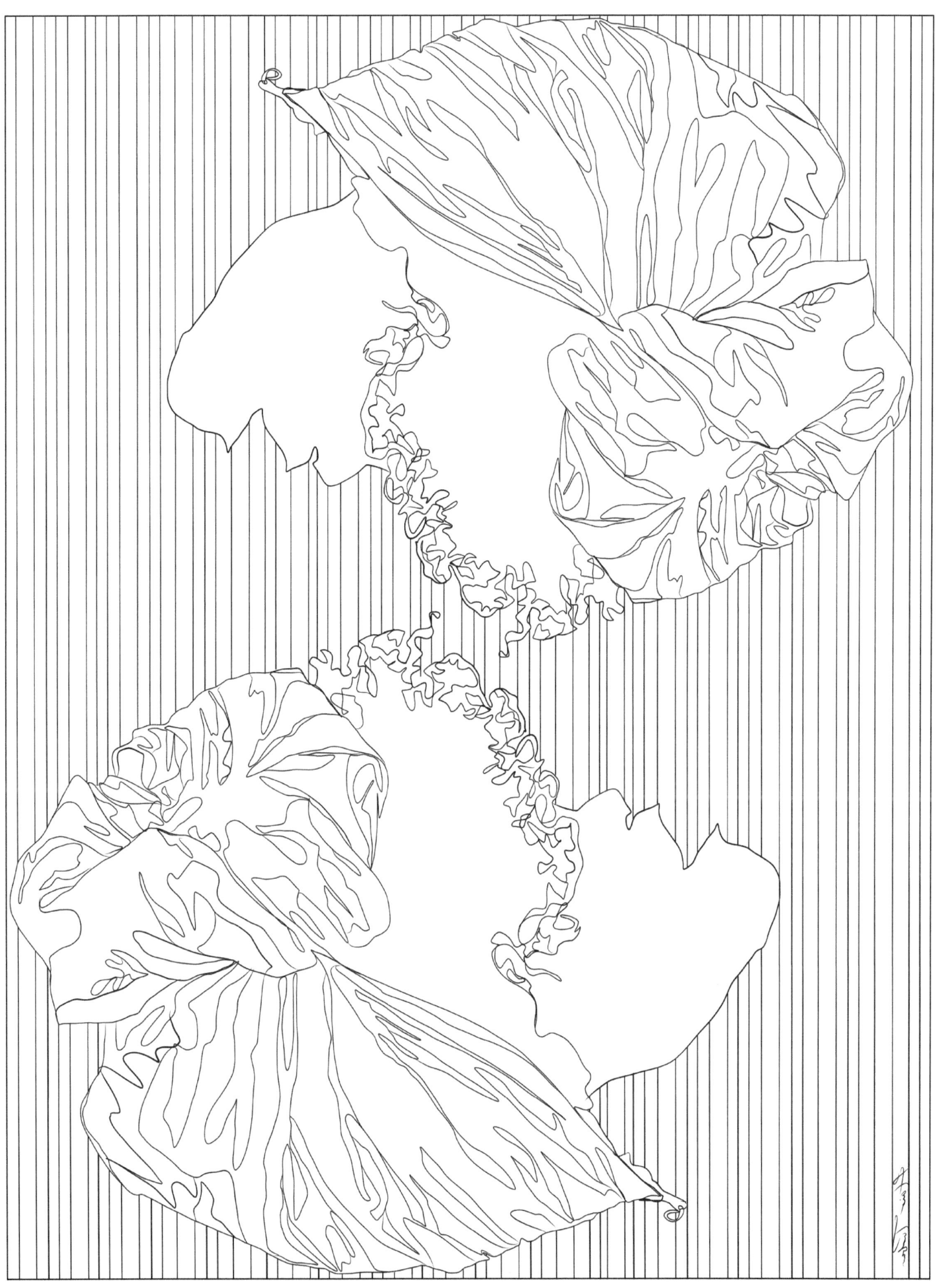

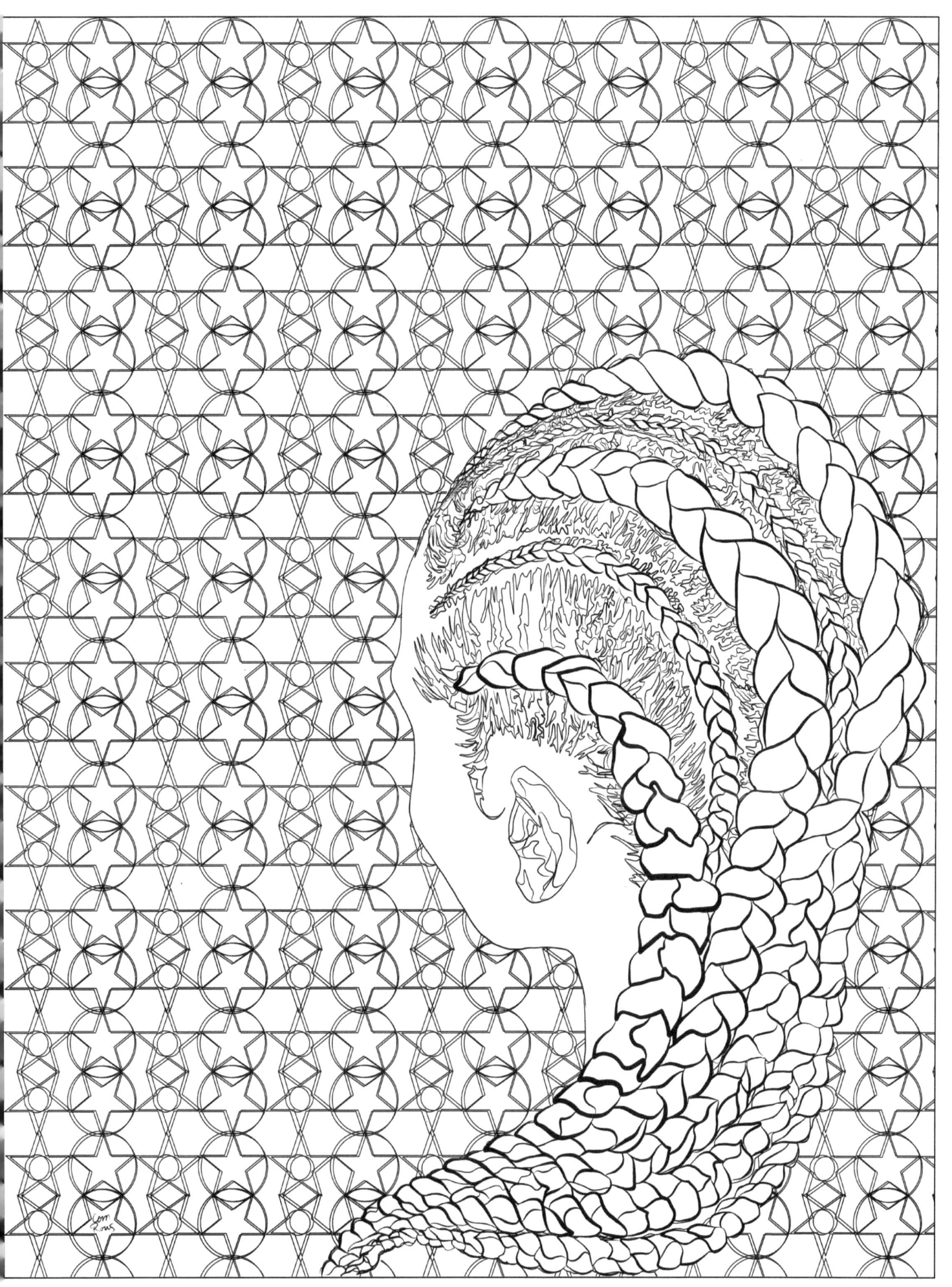

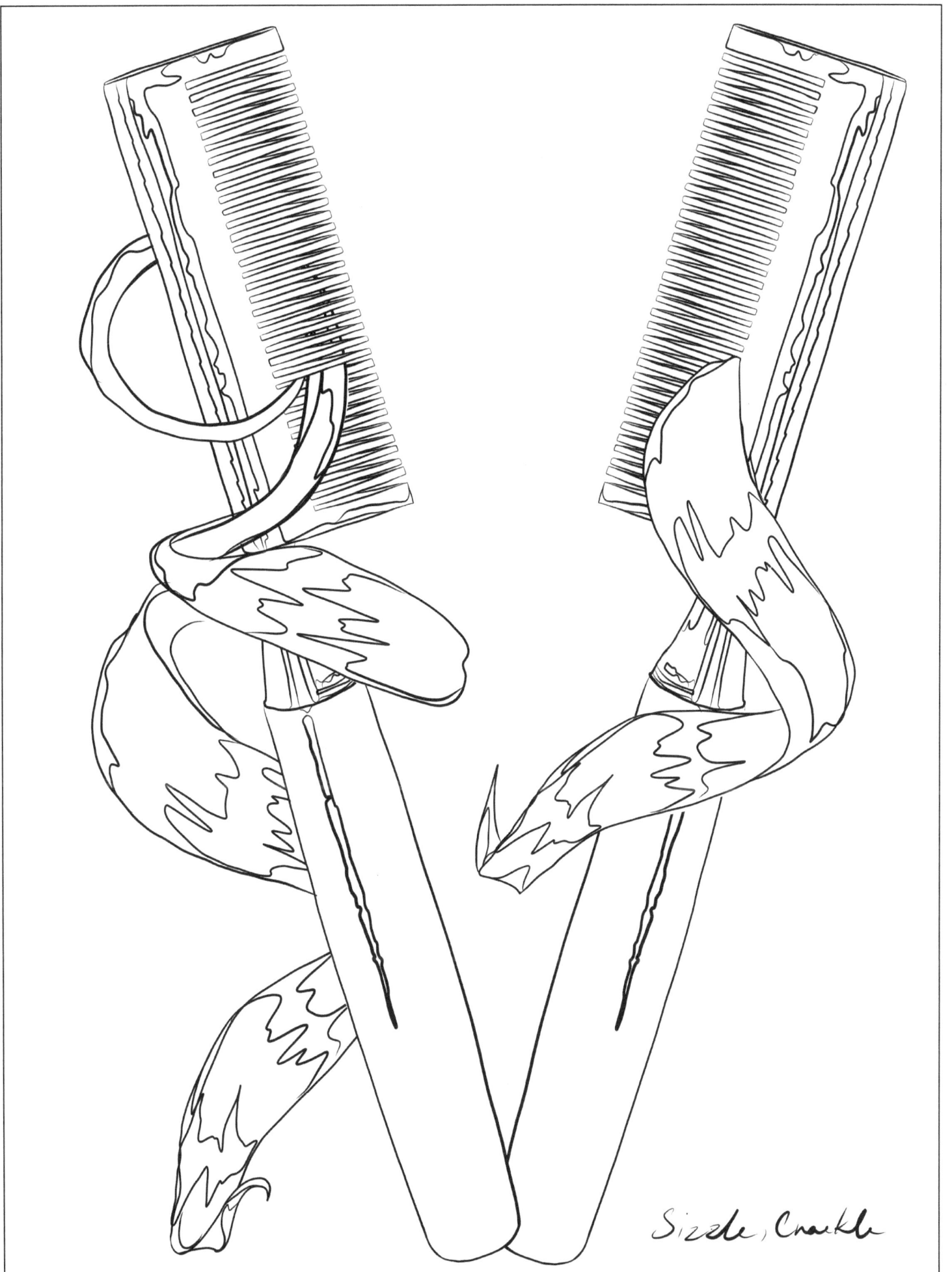

Sizzle, Crackle

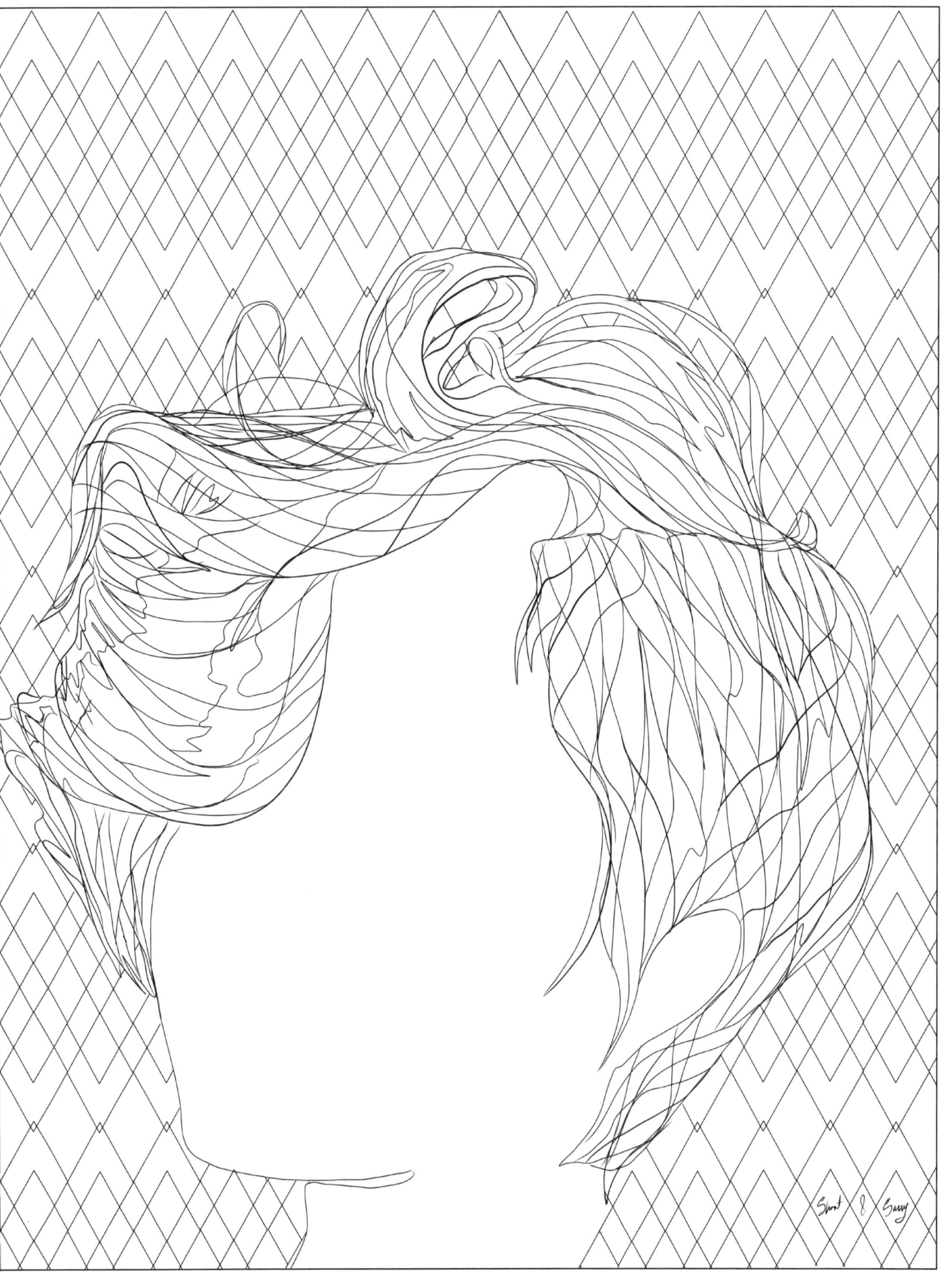

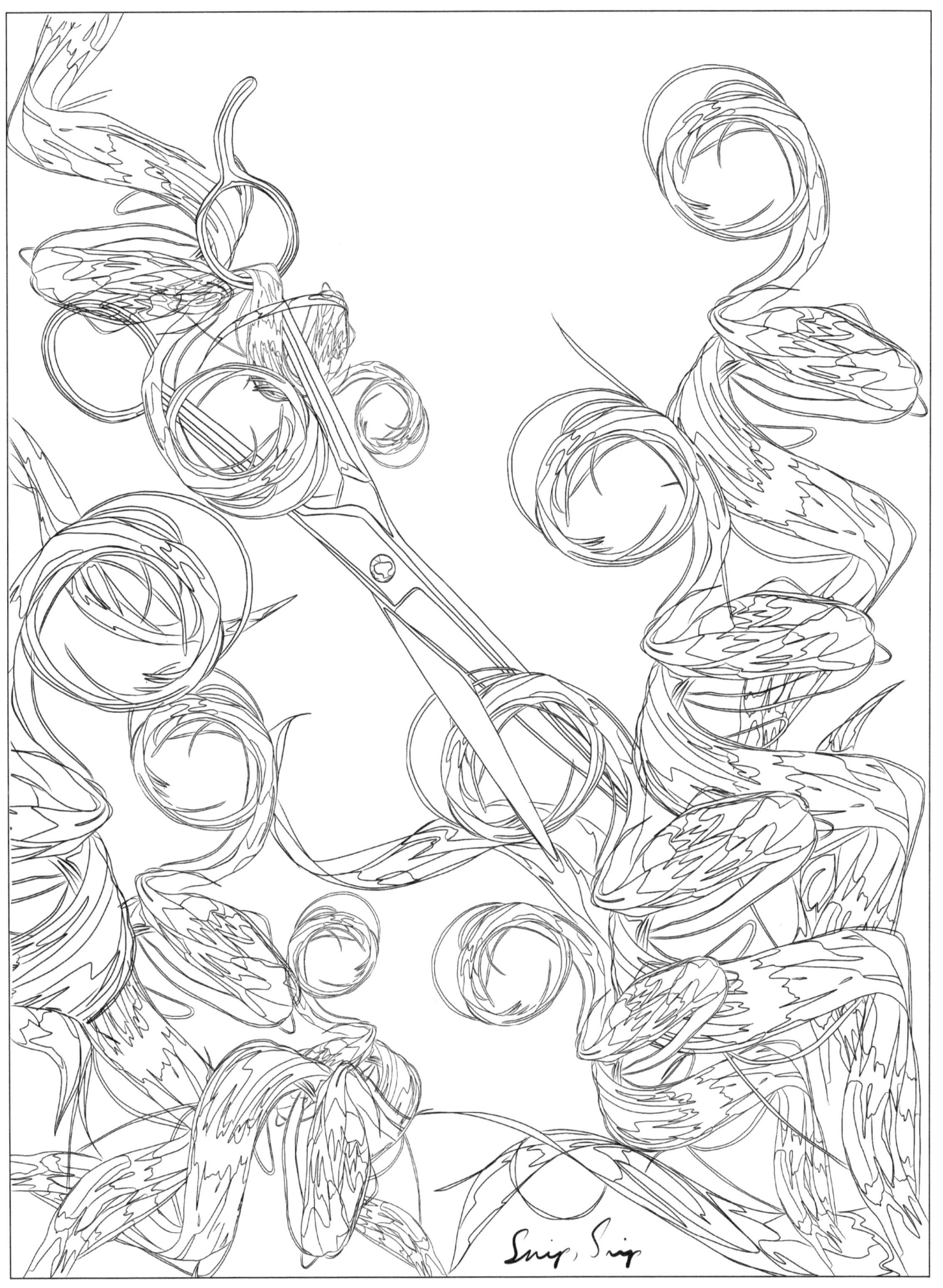

Snip, Snip

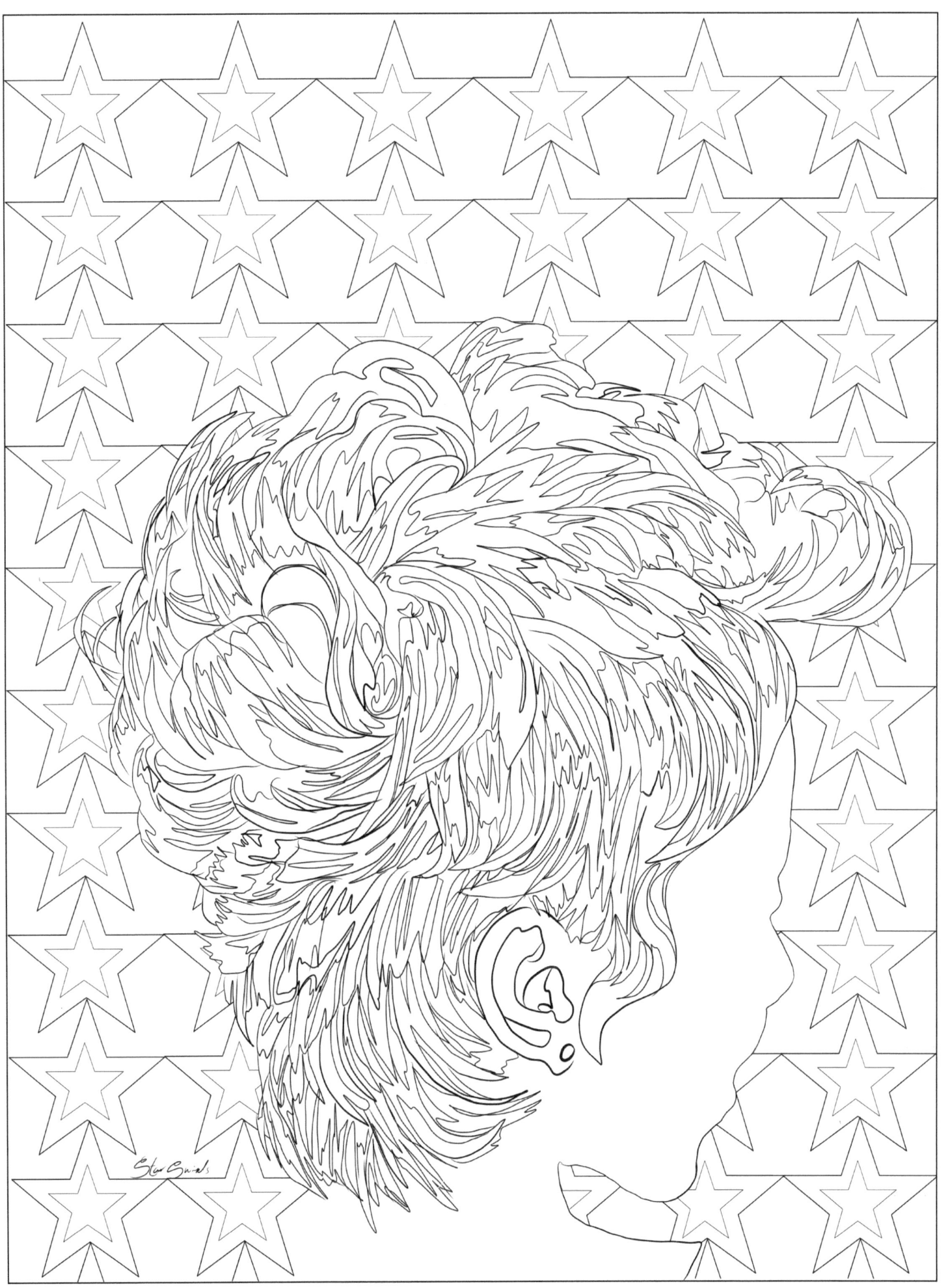

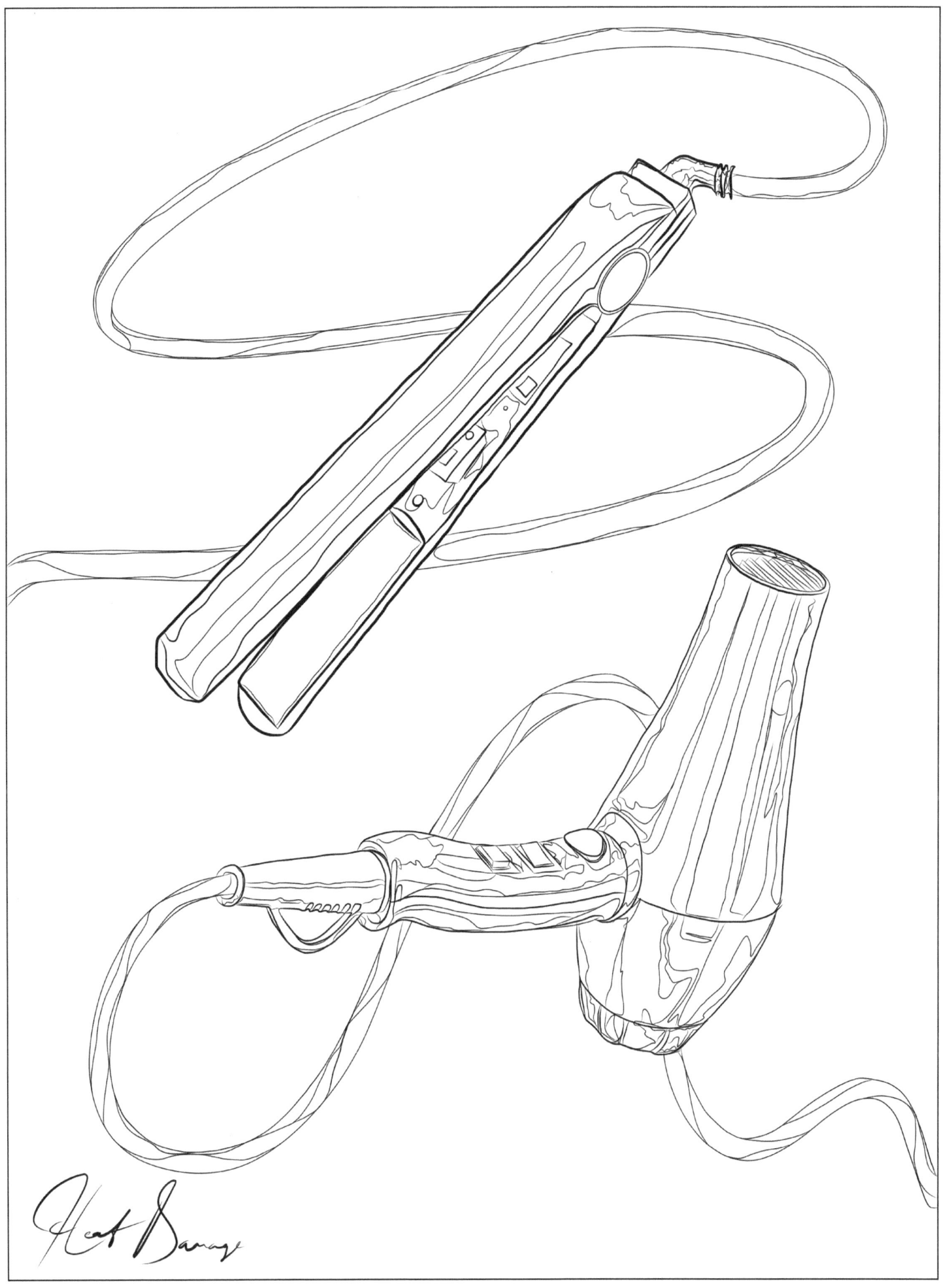

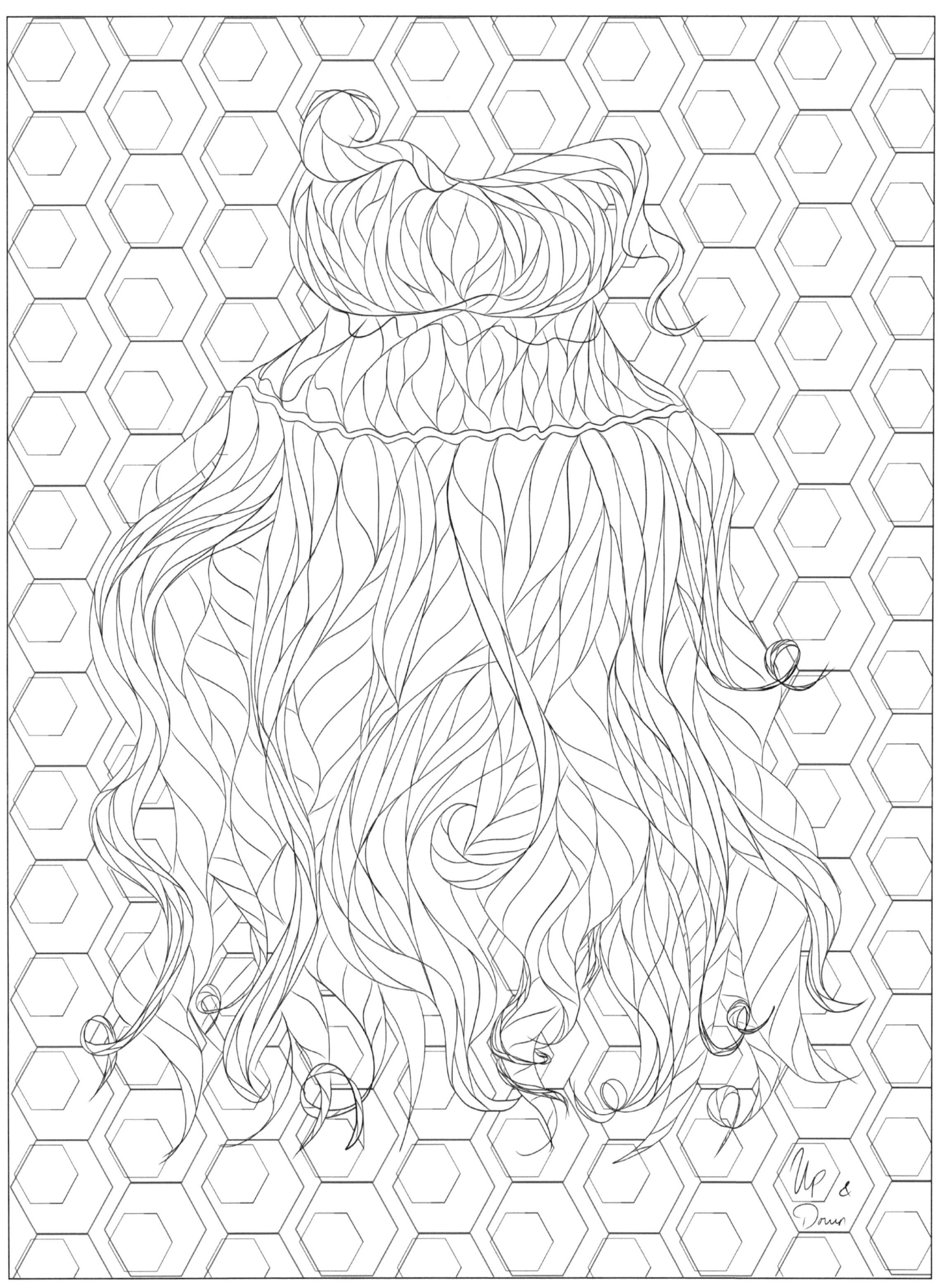

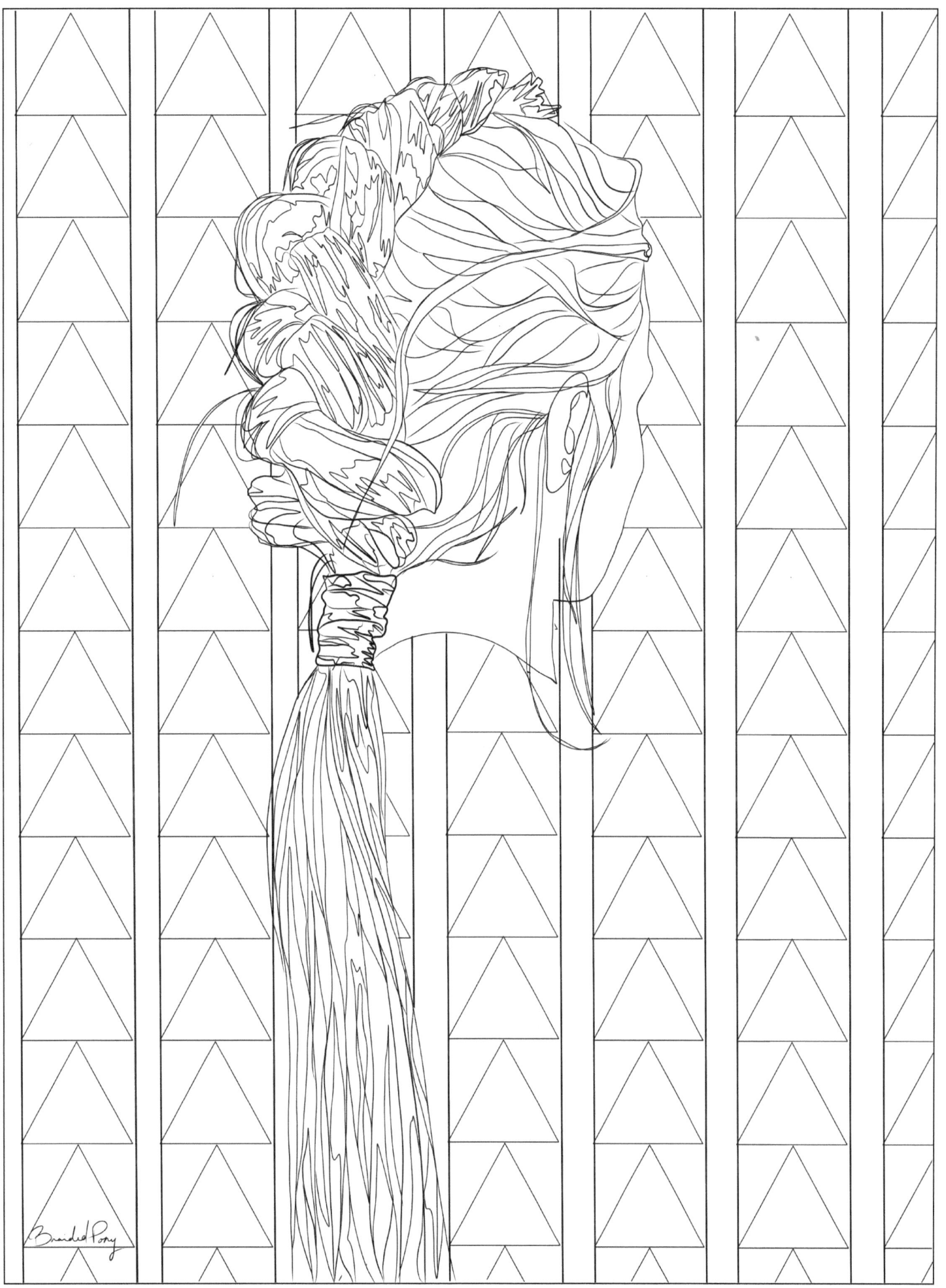

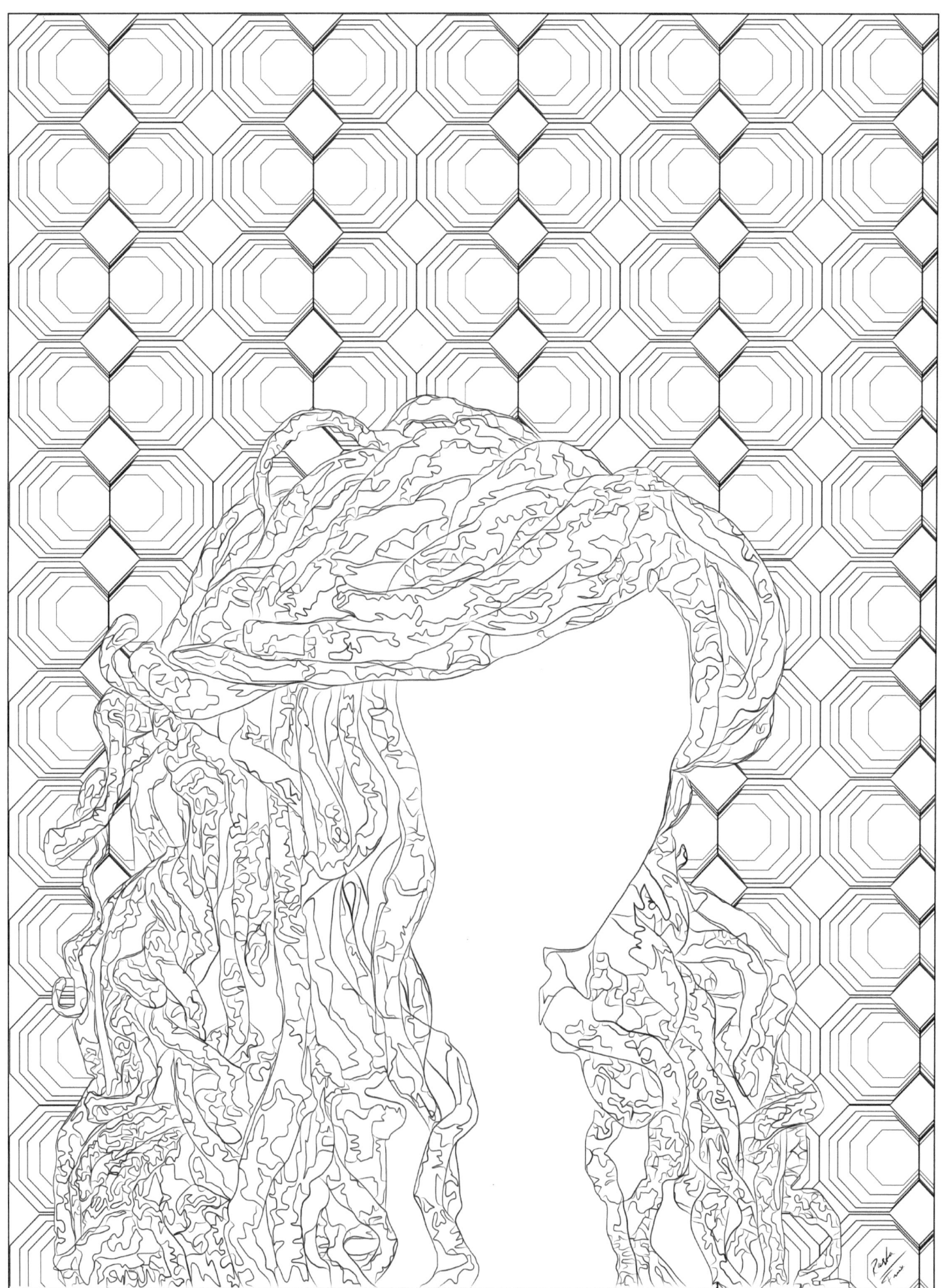

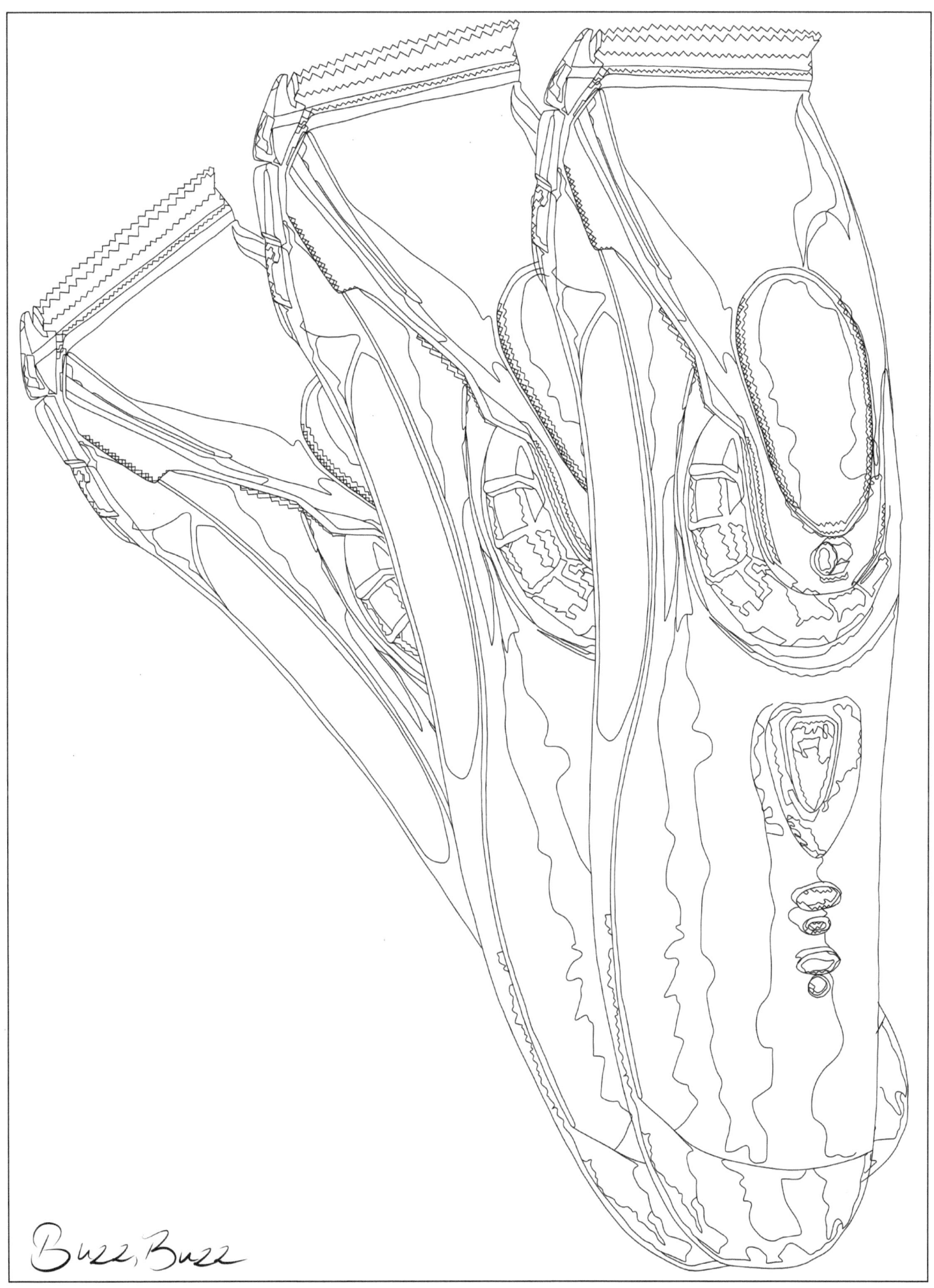

Buzz, Buzz

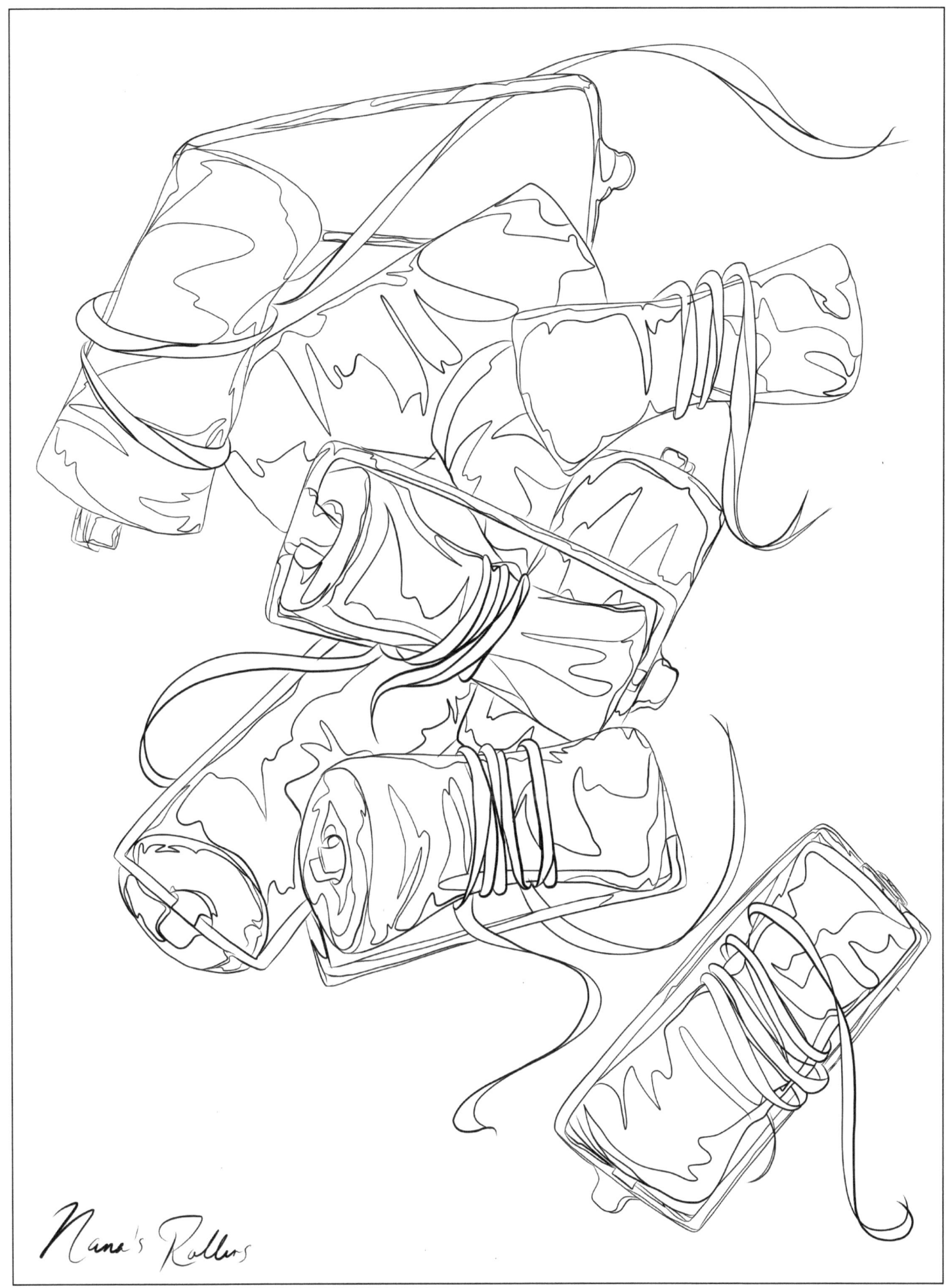

Nana's Rollers

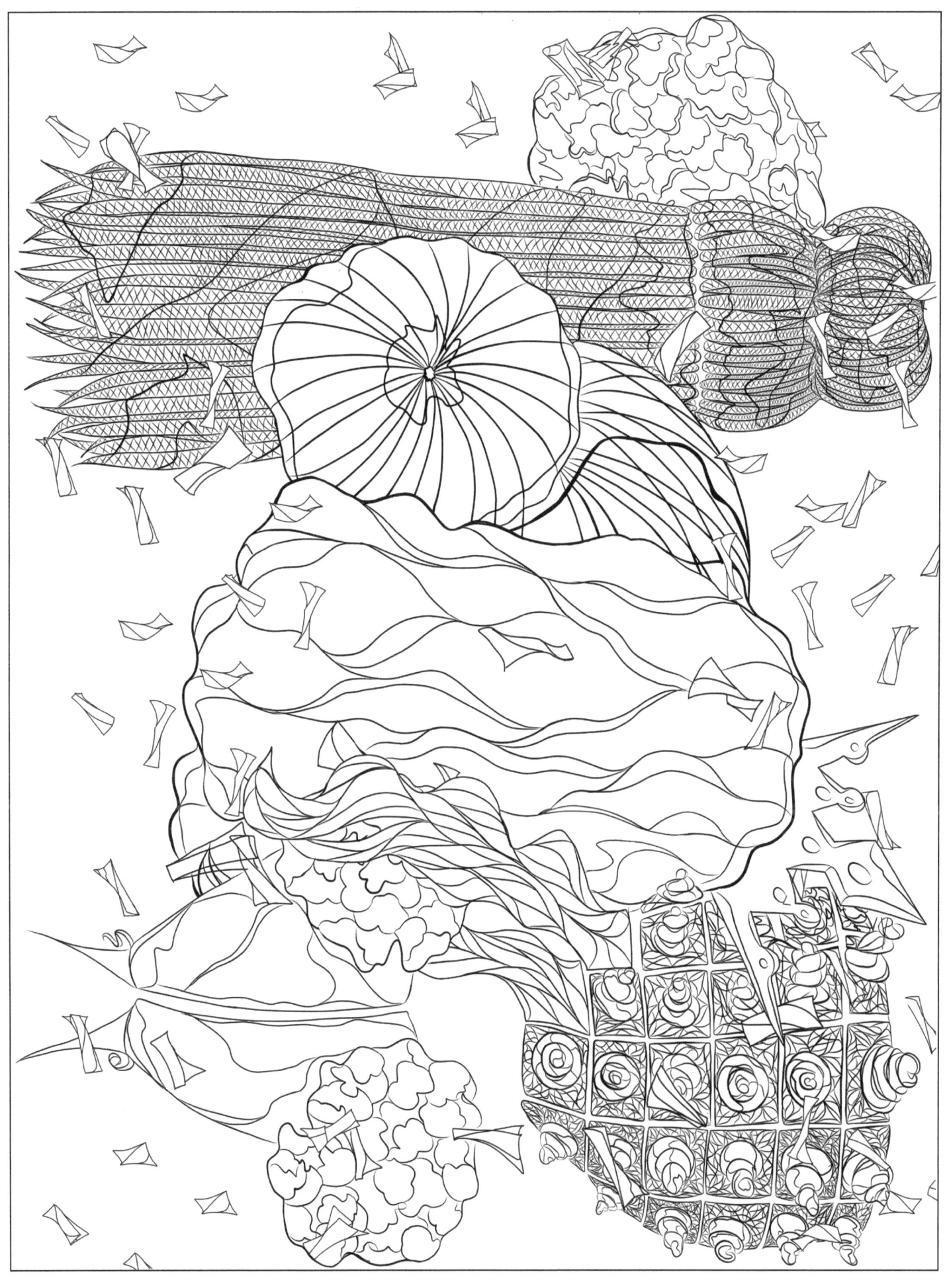